HOW TO BE FUNNY

HOW TO BE FUNNY

by Michael Townsend Smith

FAST BOOKS

For Carol Storke
the one I love

Fast Books are edited and published by Michael Smith
P. O. Box 1268, Silverton, OR 97381

ISBN 978-0-9982793-1-2

HOW TO BE FUNNY

Everything is funny.

Oh all right, nothing is funny.

Have it your own way.

Something must be funny, though.

Taking yourself seriously is frequently funny.

Nothing is serious.

Serious is dangerous.

Everything is serious.

Everything is dangerous.

Serious is funny.

You are seriously funny.

Otherwise everything is unbearably heavy.

You don't dare go outside.

Being locked in is only funny for the first few minutes.

Funny is free.

Funny frees you from the prison of self.

Self is a prison.

Nothing about prison is funny.

Prison eats time.

Time is a prison.

Hard to think of time as funny.

Self is an image.

What you think other people see is not what you see.

You bang your head on the bars.

This may be momentarily funny.

Being old is funny if you think it is.

Being old is hardly serious.

You are happy anyway.

Being comfortable is funny if you let it be.

Sitting in your chair upside down is funny.

Your chair is comfortable but you are not.

Upside down is funny.

Being old is not always comfortable.

Being comfortable means being comfortable with yourself.

At the moment you are perfectly comfortable.

This you is not all you are.

You are young and old at the same time.

You live in the eternal now.

Your mind is somewhere else.

Your mind may be going backward.

Walking backward is funny.

So is going around in circles.

Try walking backward upside down.

Few people can, old or not.

How to be funny.

Think of something so completely inappropriate that you don't dare mention it.

Dare to ignore everything that is going on in the larger world.

Dare to be funny.

Dare to be disgusting.

Disgusting is funny.

Try liking something disgusting.

Try eating it.

Maybe it is not as disgusting as you thought.

Maybe it is nourishing and delicious.

Moving quickly is funny.

Slow motion is funny.

Normal is funny.

Everything is funny.

Old people are funny.

Old people are slow.

Old people trying to go fast are funny.

Old people swimming are funny.

Old people all by themselves are sometimes sad.

Everyone is sometimes sad.

Doing tai chi is funny.

Young and old can do tai chi.

Comedy is trying to be funny.

Comedy is exhausting.

Give in to whatever it is.

Resistance is futile.

Try to think it is funny.

Join in.

🖐 🖐 🖐

How to be funny when you don't feel funny.

How to feel funny anyway.

How funny feeling funny can be.

Nothing is funny anymore.

Funny is retro.

When was the last time you thought something was funny?

Five minutes?

Laughter is a sign of funniness.

Funny is fun, fun not always funny.

Death is no fun.

Other people dying is not funny.

Neither is dying yourself.

Bad news is not funny.

Bad news is no help.

Bad news is serious.

Good news is not serious.

Good news is funny.

Bad news is reality.

Good news is fantasy.

Bad news wins.

Good will win out in the end is a funny idea.

Entertain ideas and they will entertain you.

Bad news happens in other places.

Everyone you know is fine.

Now you can be funny.

Weather is funny.

You can enjoy it even when it is "bad."

Rain is funny.

So is sunshine.

Changeable weather is especially funny.

Sometimes you don't enjoy it.

Sometimes it is inconvenient.

Too much of a good thing is not funny.

A cheerful attitude helps.

🖐 🖐 🖐

Originality is a funny idea.

How can anyone be original after all this time?

Hasn't everything already been tried?

🖐 🖐 🖐

How can anyone be original if people are all the same?

Are you the same?

Some people are funny to others.

Some people are funny to themselves.

Others are barely funny at all.

This is discrimination.

You prefer to affirm that everyone is funny.

It is all in the details.

Not all the details are different.

All suffer.

All laugh when circumstances allow.

Circumstances are not always funny.

Some circumstances are good.

Some circumstances are bad.

Either way you are alive.

If you are reading or hearing this you are alive.

You already know how to be funny.

You are still not laughing.

But there is a twinkle in your eye.

Something must be funny though you can't think what.

An airplane flying over the house is funny.

Are airplanes still funny?

The silence after the airplane passes is funny.

The roaring, whining, and crunching of the tractor outside is funny.

The tractor closely approaching and then driving away is funny.

Noise is followed by silence.

Silence is relative.

Everything is relative.

Relative is funny.

Wetting your pants is not as funny as falling into a swimming pool with your clothes on.

🖐 🖐 🖐

Bad news may be one person or many.

Terrible things happen.

Some days go better than others.

History is not music.

Reality is individual bodies.

Experience is inside them.

What a relief if you could sleep all the time!

Try to wake up.

🖐 🖐 🖐

How to be funny.

Say the word.

Play with a three-year-old.

Think about nothing else.

Want nothing for yourself.

Three-year-olds are funny.

Three-year-olds wear you out.

You want something more.

It will be funny when the time comes.

You'll see.

Writing is funny.

Funny-ha ha or funny-peculiar?

How to get from the latter to the former.

How to be funny-ha ha.

How come you never stand on your head anymore?

You are afraid to try.

You are afraid to be upside down.

You are afraid something will break.

You are afraid to be backward.

You are afraid to be inside out.

You are afraid of everything.

No, really, you are not afraid of anything.

You laugh at danger until you find yourself in it.

Ha ha.

Too late.

Putting things off till tomorrow is funny.

Mañana is funnier still.

Mexicans have more fun.

You can't do everything at once.

Multi-tasking is funny up to a point.

Anyway you need something to do tomorrow.

Something to do is something to look forward to.

Looking forward to something gives you something to look forward to.

How to be funny.

Smile as if you had a secret.

Secrets are funny.

Get that mischievous look in your eye.

Mischief is funny or annoying according to your immediate state of mind.

Or the other person's state of mind.

Watch out!

The secret may be something you haven't happened to mention.

Or something you don't want anyone to know.

Or don't dare talk about.

Or promised someone you would never reveal.

Someone else's secret is not yours to betray.

If information is currency shouldn't you be spending more?

A secret may be a secret from yourself, like where you hid the key so you can find it when you need it.

Is there anything funny about this?

It is all funny.

Take my word for it is funny.

Thinking about what you never talk about is funny.

Everyone has an inner life.

Otherwise nothing is funny.

In order for anything to be funny, it has to exist.

In order for anything to exist, there has to be a word.

Thinking is another word for talking to yourself.

Can you think without words?

Supposedly there are other kinds of thinking.

Words can be funny and make you laugh.

Funny words include rutabaga, swede, turnip, and neep, all meaning the same thing.

How are things different from their words?

Nonsense is funny unless it has serious consequences.

Some people don't realize they are talking nonsense.

Serious people think they are making sense.

Sense is not typically funny.

Letting go of sense opens the door to something else.

Possibly funny.

Or it could make the situation much worse.

🖐 🖐 🖐

Mental illness is not funny.

Being crazy is only funny if you are not crazy.

Funny people are often crazy.

Being crazy is doing crazy things.

All people are crazy in one way or another.

Dreams are crazy.

People are funny when they can't stand not to be.

Nothing is better.

Some people are funny for money.

Money is funny if you can afford it.

Funny money is fun.

Some people have too much money to be funny.

Having no money is funny if more is on the way.

Otherwise having no money is not funny.

You would be crazy to think it is.

How to be funny when everything is going to hell.

Clichés may have been funny the first time.

Try to take them literally.

Exceptions are funny.

Anything you say could be the opposite of what you mean.

You can say what you mean but no one wants to hear it.

It is too funny, and they are trying to be serious.

Complicated thoughts are funny.

That you are an exception, for example.

You are more typical than you think.

You are not exceptional like Beethoven or Napoleon.

There is nothing complicated about that.

Waiting for your genius to be recognized is funny.

Genius wants to be recognized at the time.

Not being recognized is not funny if you take yourself seriously.

Beethoven took himself seriously and was often funny, Napoleon often serious.

You are exceptional in other ways.

This is important.

You are the only one of something, and someone should notice.

If you don't take yourself seriously, who will?

You don't have to be funny.

How to be funny if you are itching all over your body, for instance.

How to be funny if things have gone irretrievably wrong.

Dare to be funny again.

Trying to be funny is funny when people agree to think it is.

Making a fool of yourself is a good way to be funny.

People like seeing people make fools of themselves.

Letting other people know what you are trying to do is asking to be misunderstood.

Trying and failing to be funny is embarrassing.

Disappointment is more poignant than funny.

Satisfaction doesn't have to be funny.

Embarrassment is funny unless you are seriously embarrassed.

Being misunderstood is funny.

Everyone is misunderstood.

Children are funny.

Children like to play.

Grown-ups are too busy.

Grown-ups like to kill.

Kind people kill flies and spiders as a personal favor.

Is that true?

Everybody likes to kill something.

Is that true?

Everybody likes to play and laugh and have fun.

Flies are annoying.

Spiders bite.

Mosquitoes stab innocent children with their needle-sharp proboscis.

Think of what you had to put up with when you were a child.

Chiggers.

Leeches.

Ticks.

Cooties.

Children like to be alive.

Bugs are alive.

🖐 🖐 🖐

Emotions are funny.

You pretend not to have emotions or that they don't matter, give way to them in moments of extremity or try to control them and not fall apart, wonder what you are supposed to be feeling, wonder what you actually are feeling, misunderstand other people's emotions, misrepresent your own, wish you could be more sincere and expressive and let your friends in on what you are feeling.

Instead they talk about themselves.

You edit your emotions.

Don't worry, be happy.

You want people to recognize and respect your emotions even when they are uncomfortable and inconvenient.

Other people's emotions are not funny even if you think they are.

You can recognize that someone is experiencing an emotion and still not think it makes any sense.

That may not be good enough.

It isn't necessarily funny just because you think it's ridiculous.

You want to feel positive emotions, love, acceptance, tenderness, desire, pleasure, satisfaction, bliss.

Or you want to die.

You are joking.

Not really.

If it isn't comedy or farce, it is drama or tragedy.

Comedy and farce are funny, drama and tragedy

generally not.

There is also dramatic comedy and tragic farce.

Which do you think is funnier?

Think about it.

Is that a definite opinion?

People are funny even if they don't think they are.

They have their little ways.

Little ways are funny.

Step aside and let them do it.

Try not to laugh at them or take it personally.

Or do laugh.

They may be trying to make you laugh.

Time is going by.

They do what they do just as you do what you do.

If you think it is funny, it is.

How to be funny if you still don't feel funny.

Feeling funny can be a sign of something that isn't funny.

Feeling funny should be taken seriously if you feel seriously funny.

Doctors rely on tests.

These are not the same tests you learned to deal with in school.

Doctors are not teachers.

Changing the subject is funny as a last resort.

Repetition is funny.

Anything is funny if you repeat it enough times

This may not include the things you do over and over all the time.

You don't even think about it.

Are they funny if you do?

You are a machine.

Machines are funny.

They do one thing over and over.

They break down and need to be repaired.

They may become obsolete when they are still working perfectly well.

Nothing lasts forever.

Laughter is a form of speech.

Laughing is a personality.

Laughing is a mannerism.

Laughing is a way of not being serious even if you are serious.

Laughing too much is okay if the other person is laughing too.

Being funny is harder.

Being funny makes other people laugh.

Laughing makes people feel better about the situation without necessarily doing anything to change the situation.

Laughing annoys people who don't see what's so funny.

Feeling better is better.

Don't hold back.

Holding back is not funny.

Going too far is funny until you go too far.

Dead-pan is not always funny.

You could just be holding back.

You could stop trying to be funny.

If it is your fate not to be funny, it is probably no use trying to change it.

Laugh out loud at people's funny stories if you can without embarrassing yourself.

Laughing at people's funny stories makes them like you.

Tell funny stories so people will remember how much they like you.

Unfortunately you seldom think of funny stories at appropriate moments.

When you manage to come out with one it is not as funny as you thought it would be.

People like you anyway, but possibly not as much as they would if you were funnier.

How to be funny.

Puns.

Jokes.

Coincidences.

Funny faces.

Funny voices.

Funny walks.

Crossed eyes.

Pretending to be drunk.

Falling down and pretending to have a fit.

It doesn't matter that you are not funny.

No one has to be funny.

🖐 🖐 🖐

Everyone talking at the same time is funny.

Flying across the country to spend two days with your family is funny if you don't get sick.

Chinese is funny.

White American is funny.

Being yourself is funny.

Taking yourself seriously, as you know.

Eating weird food.

Flying across the ocean to eat, drink, and speak Spanish or Italian.

Badminton.

All funny.

A certain amount of natural hilarity arises just from

being together.

Whatever you say, someone will think it is funny.

Horses whinnying is funny.

Cocks crowing is funny.

You may as well think everything is funny.

You may as well laugh if you can.

Sometimes you want to be serious though.

That's all right.

Some things are serious.

Leukemia and pneumonia are serious and mysterious.

Complications are serious but may still be funny from a funny point of view.

Loved ones with complications are an opportunity to be useful.

Being funny can be useful but may not always be appropriate.

They may not feel funny.

If you feel funny it is probably nothing.

When to be serious.

Do something even if it is not funny.

Something is not always better than nothing.

Why is there anything?

🖐 🖐 🖐

Can you go on?

You must go on until you figure out how to be funny.

Then you can be funny or not according to the situation and your own inclinations at the time.

Your pants falling down is funny.

Your wig falling off is funny, though probably not to you.

Falling down is funny if you don't hurt yourself.

Stepping in a hole is usually not funny.

"If" is funny.

There is no if.

There is only what is.

Redefine it as you will.

Fun-house mirrors are funny.

You can't stop laughing.

You never want to leave.

Seeing double is funny.

Falling asleep is funny.

Being asleep when you think you are awake is funny.

Dreaming that you have risen and started your day and realizing you are still in bed and haven't moved is funny.

All sorts of funny things, known or not, coexist with you in the thin film of atmosphere cloaking your stony shivering planet, not to even mention the limitless beyond.

Cross-dressing is funny.

Gender is funny.

The idea that you have to be one thing or another is funny.

This or that anything is funny.

Everything is much more fluid than that.

Sex is funny.

Fluid can be exchanged any number of ways.

Plato was right about that.

Clothes in general are funny.

It's funny that you have to wear anything.

What you wear is a costume that unavoidably signifies something.

You no longer worry about the impression you are making, you just want to wear clothes you like.

Being naked used to be funny.

As for other people's clothes, at best you take note and move on.

Bodies too.

Clothes are fun.

Take a chance.

Wear something funny.

Go ahead and be ridiculous.

Everyone else is.

You have no interest in cross-dressing, unless you do.

You would like a suit covered in flowers.

Sex is another story.

Nothing funny stays the same.

Everything changes, sometimes too soon, sometimes not soon enough.

🖐 🖐 🖐

Do you feel complete in yourself?

You could be if you had to.

It might not be funny.

So you have sex.

Sex is serious.

You activate your body and forget everything else.

You give yourself to the other and forget who you are.

All that and an orgasm too.

It may not be funny at the time.

It is hard to be simultaneously funny and turned on.

How you feel afterward is not the same as how you felt in the act.

Sex is an act.

You do it or you would like to do it or you used to like to do it and may want to do it again if the proper situation arises.

Acting is funny.

Anything you do will lead to something else.

If you don't do anything, something will happen anyway and not be your doing.

Even if you act, something unforeseen will happen eventually.

Unintended consequences are funny as long as no one gets hurt.

🖐 🖐 🖐

Sunlight is funny.

Darkness is funny if you are a night person.

Darkness doesn't have to be funny or not funny, it can be exciting, seductive, comforting, a relief or a refreshing contrast, deeply frightening, opportunity for mischief, and anything else you may or may not think of.

Sunlight makes plants grow.

It warms you and enables you to see.

Everything is still there in the dark.

The stars are still there in the daytime.

In the dark you can only see things light is shining on or from, a particular stochastic subset of all the funny things you see in daylight.

It seems to be a different world although it is actually the same.

🖐 🖐 🖐

When the time comes you will go.

Funny how you make plans and then do them.

Funny how you can plan ahead.

You think of yourself as spontaneous, but what you expect to happen usually does.

You do what you intended to do with the results you expected.

There may be no really funny surprises for months at a time.

How to be free.

Telling funny stories is funny.

Being funny is what makes them stories.

The whole point is to make people laugh.

If people laugh they will like you even if they think you are ridiculous and are merely humoring you.

They won't be able to stop watching you even if they realize you are evil.

Going through the motions is funny.

Events may be restructured for the sake of funniness.

The truth may be stretched.

Everyone agrees that's okay but not when you are running for president.

Outrageous opinions are often funny but may be dangerously ill-informed.

The whole spectacle would be funny if it weren't such a nightmare.

No one is laughing anymore.

This is no time to be funny.

Stephen Colbert is funny.

Whoopie Goldberg is serious.

When Whoopie Goldberg is serious something is seriously wrong.

How can you not like her?

Or him?

Fame is funny that way.

If you are famous and disappear you can make a comeback.

If you are good you can go on being good, although you may never be as good as you used to be.

You are not as smart as you were age ten.

Whatever made you famous might have been the high point.

The rest is exploitation and trying to be real.

Famous is all the time.

You don't get to leave it at the office.

If you are funny enough someone will notice.

It keeps you on your toes.

You'd better have some funny stories up your nose.

You are slowly making progress in learning how to be funny.

Looking at people doing funny things is funny.

Some move faster than others

People who walk faster live longer.

They see you looking at them.

They say, "What?"

Or would if they were paying attention.

It's funny how people match each other's tempi.

People moving at a different tempo seem to be weirdly out of it and potentially dangerous.

Hurry up, you think, or not so fast.

Speeding cars are especially dangerous.

Danger can be exhilarating, even sexy, or substitute

for sex.

People who look for danger can easily find it.

If you laugh at danger you are asking for trouble.

Danger is not funny even if you think it is.

Danger is real.

Reality is sometimes funny, sometimes decidedly not.

There are many aspects of contemporary life you would rather not think about.

Complex questions that have no answers.

There is nothing to be done short of giving up everything and throwing yourself bodily beneath the wheels of the juggernaut.

It's a funny situation.

Summer is funny, the way it is hot for a couple of days and then not.

Nights are cool as if you were further north than you actually are.

Style is funny.

Enough, in the sense of just right, is funny.

Style is not enough.

You shouldn't have to die afterwards.

A good movie doesn't kill you.

Something has to happen.

Something does happen, but life is not art.

Form is a property of art, not life.

Art copying life makes it make more sense than it actually does.

Life is not a novel, as you were formerly tempted to imagine, although it has a beginning and middle and eventually will end.

Life is not a sonata but like a sonata has principal and secondary themes and development in the middle.

Recapitulation is optional.

In the absence of a director, playwright, composer, or conductor, nobody is doing it but you.

You have to be funny yourself.

If someone else is there and joins in, so much the better.

Other people are funny.

Everyone has a funny personality he or she is not willing or able to change.

You are not allowed to laugh in their face.

They are serious about it even when they are kidding around.

Earnestly being themselves.

Making it up as you go along is funny.

Groping in the dark is funny.

Stubbing your toe is funny unless you have broken it.

Pain is funny in small doses.

You are too sensitive.

Every little thing makes an impression.

Accidents are lying in wait.

Falling off a horse is funny when you are young.

Wipe your nose and come back for more.

Slapping someone you love is not funny.

Everything is changed.

That was funny, you think afterward.

What did I do?

Being alone is funny during daylight hours.

Other people add necessary complications.

It's funny how complicated it is.

If you don't do something nothing good will come of it.

It's like winding a clock.

The clock is a reminder from earlier generations that you have to keep winding a clock.

Otherwise it runs down.

The chiming of the hours and halves is heard no more.

Other people have their own clocks if they are lucky.

"If" is still funny.

Luck is funny.

Is there such a thing as luck or is it all just random?

Getting high is funny at first.

Everything changes.

Everything goes on moving although you are not moving.

That warm glow spreading through your body is a

funny idea whose time has come.

Thinking whatever anyone says is funny is funny.

You come up with brilliant thoughts no one ever had before.

No one else is like you.

That there are 7.4 billion people and no two alike is funny.

Chinese are all alike.

Arab terrorists are all alike, etc.

Just kidding.

Kidding is funny.

Seriously, no one is like you or anyone else.

What can you say to someone who doesn't like you?

Don't you mean *isn't* like you?

No one ever knows exactly what you mean.

You can be funny by yourself but you feel silly laughing by yourself.

You sound like one of your parents.

Contractions are funny, aren't they.

Using contractions is pretending you're talking.

Writing is a form of talking, although talking is not writing.

No two of anything are funny in the same way.

Comedy is funny because we agree it is.

Getting lost is funny until you realize you are really lost.

You understand the words but not why people are saying them.

Explaining is an exercise in futility.

You might as well be talking to yourself.

Waste the whole day.

Don't bother to be funny.

Time keeps going by even when you do nothing.

The sun slowly moves across the sky.

Evening shadows fall.

Twilight lingers.

Stars and the moon appear.

They were there all the time.

So were you.

Existence is no joke.

Much of the time God is not kidding.

That doesn't mean you have to be serious.

You are not in charge of everything.

You are only in charge of yourself.

Do not let your mind wander when you need to be paying attention.

Do not fuck up.

Fucking up is not funny.

No mistakes is better than hapless bumbling.

No one is perfect but not for want of trying.

You don't have to be funny if you don't feel like being funny.

You may still want to be funny, though, because beauty loses its novelty, and happiness is a steady state, and you could use a few laughs.

Earth, a smallish planet, is huge in relation to one person.

There are a huge number of people in relation to the one of you.

How funny is that!?

There are more people than you realize.

They are everywhere, like cockroaches.

Fourteen cockroaches costumed as English aristocrats sit down to dinner in the baronial dining hall, attended by cockroaches uniformed as footmen.

Many of them like to gather in crowds.

Others can't stand crowds and avoid them despite being convinced that mass protest is the only way anything is going to change.

It doesn't usually work out even so.

Here at home it is more a matter of regularity.

Decide how you want to live and put systems in place to make it possible.

One way or another you manage to get what you need and most of what you want.

How to make it funny.

Trash lies waiting for you to remove it.

Weeds dare you to dig them up.

Chicken shit piles up.

It's ridiculous.

Funny is something else.

🖐 🖐 🖐

Intensity of attitude is funny.

You need it to get anything done, but stress doesn't help.

Get over it.

Go on to something else.

Then come back.

Art demands patience.

Inspiration arises of its own accord.

Allow and promulgate continuity of intention.

Funniness helps.

Funny how the broad fields so recently green have now turned tawny.

The harvest is in.

🖐 🖐 🖐

Business never ends.

It will feed you.

It will eat you.

Put it in a box or cage and don't let it out however much it promises to change and never hit you again.

Grow or die.

🖐 🖐 🖐

Horror is a funny thing to like.

What kind of person enjoys seeing people being terrified and then dismembered?

Stage blood is still blood.

Murder mysteries are a funny kind of story to be so popular.

Finding out who did it doesn't automatically make it funny.

🖐 🖐 🖐

How to be funny.

Pretend you don't speak the language.

How is that funny?

Analyze how weirdly people speak.

Unusually high and low voices are funny.

Variant vowel and consonant sounds are fascinating in themselves.

Language isn't everything, even so.

Largeness and smallness are equally funny.

Chihuahuas and miniature horses are funny.

Whales are funny.

Whales' large slow thoughts are nothing like your small fast thoughts, although adjusted for size and environment they are equally funny.

You have large thoughts too.

Sometimes your small thoughts are slow.

Sometimes you try to think and can't.

Sometimes you try not to think and can't stop.

Which is worse?

Mathematics is funny.

Everything adds up.

You can know for certain whether you are right or wrong.

Trying to get something done is funny.

Seconds go by, minutes, hours, days, months, years.

Things come in the mail that you feel you have to open.

Email is funny.

There it is.

You learn a whole new way of functioning.

Everything is the same but different, likewise different but the same.

Nothing is the same even though it goes on more or less the same way day after day for decades.

Centuries.

Before that everything was different.

Men with clubs dragging women around by the hair was considered to be hilarious.

Dinosaurs were funny when they were not killing you.

Giants are funny when they are not stomping through your vegetable garden.

Ogres are funny when you are not the one trying to cross the bridge.

Fleas are funny when you are not the one they are biting.

Cave people scratching flea bites is not funny.

Feeling sorry for people who have never even heard of electricity and running water is ridiculous.

What are you going to do about it?

How to be funny.

Make something funny for dinner.

Food is funny.

People putting what they think of as food into their mouths, chewing and swallowing, washing it down with a swig of wine, waving their hands in the air and talking emphatically at the same time is funny.

So is looking out the window.

Two cats wrestling in the grass have their arms around each other like lovers.

One is biting the other's throat.

Cats are funny.

People love to watch them.

Complicated lives are funny.

Cats' lives are not as complicated as yours.

Yours might be as simple as theirs, except no one is bringing you food and water and cleaning up your poop.

Feeding animals is funny.

Each species eats in its own way.

Feeling lost and empty is not funny.

Sweeping the floor will help.

It is not hot yet.

You are not actually paralyzed.

Everything doesn't have to be funny.

Louis C.K. doesn't have to be funny anymore.

People are comic actors whether they realize it or not.

They can be funny if they want to be funny.

Wringing your hands because they itch is funny.

You wring your hands as if something awful has happened and you can't do anything about it so you wring your hands.

It doesn't really help, but it feels so good it is hard to stop.

Stop!

Scratching your elbow and upper arm is almost as bad.

The itch-relief gel stings.

46

Getting through the day is funny.

Swim later when shade is on the pool.

That will be lovely.

🖐 🖐 🖐

The real you is naked.

You are not someone who defines him or herself by what they wear, with a signature cap, or a period look, say 1930s Berlin, that they perfect and stop at.

Any costume you put on implies a character, which requires some consistency to be credible.

Wear it sincerely, not too ironically or too seriously.

You could put on something funny for a change.

You don't have to be funny all the time.

🖐 🖐 🖐

Change the record, or the subject, or the parties.

Underclothes are still clothes.

Under the underclothes is you.

It is too hot to be naked.

Light clothes protect you from the heat.

They can be funny even if you aren't.

Hot weather is funny.

No need for clothes.

It is too hot to do anything, even naked.

🖐 🖐 🖐

To be or not to be is funny.

Everything depends on who you are.

But you don't know who you are or what it actually means to be, or not.

Opinions differ.

It doesn't matter who's right, if anyone ever is.

Opinions are funny.

Taking them seriously is funny.

Getting yourself worked up and marshalling your logic is funny.

Thinking forty-nine percent of your fellow citizens are tragically deluded is funny.

You can't help thinking what you think, though.

Your circumstances and opinions are who you are.

You are driven to articulate your thoughts if you can, witness to them if you can find a sympathetic ear, write them down, post them on the web.

You are who you are and can't help it.

Surely there are good reasons for your irrational decisions.

They are sensible and correct, or at least your own, regardless of the relentless commercial manipulation that is so much a funny part of everyday life that you don't even notice it anymore.

Do you drive your car or does it drive you?

🖐 🖐 🖐

How to be funny.

Be yourself.

Your struggle is plainly comic.

Tragedy is reserved for royalty and archetypes.

All drama is comedy in the end, after the sadness.

Sometimes it slips over into farce, too ridiculous to be believed.

Capsizing canoes are funny if everyone knows how to swim.

Be grateful.

Prepare to get wet.

🖐 🖐 🖐

Water fights are funny.

Food fights are funny.

Pillow fights are funny.

Other kinds of fights are not funny.

🖐 🖐 🖐

Getting along is better than funny.

Unless you have something to be serious about, there is no need to be so serious.

Dubious statements are not serious.

All statements are dubious.

Seriousness doesn't necessarily help.

Positive spin may help.

Spin is funny.

Spin until you fall down.

Falling down is funny when you are little and close to the floor.

Getting along depends on saying what you mean, or at least meaning what you say.

Not everything you mean can or needs to be said.

Intentions are tricky, i.e., funny.

Kisses are the language of love.

🖐 🖐 🖐

Saying the same thing over and over is funny.

Words lose their meaning if you repeat them often enough.

Speaking is not as serious or funny as writing.

Speaking falsely implies a script, which falsely implies a writer hidden in another room.

Meaning is not what you say, after all, but what you intend by saying it.

Written words are small groupings of simple signs.

Spoken words are subtle modulations of humming, tonguing, lip-smacking, and breath.

Reading silently to yourself induces unconscious ghost movements of the mouth and throat.

Language can be invisible like perfectly clear glass.

Meaning shines through.

Too smooth, it lulls you to sleep.

Polished, it can shine.

Sleep lets your brain let go and reset.

Dreams are fantastic adventures you only sometimes remember.

An unexpected word jolts you awake.

Everything is microscopically detailed.

A banjo is funnier than anything you can say.

Just the word mandolin is funny.

Funny can be beautiful also.

Funny can tell you everything you need to know.

Not thinking anything is funny is funny.

Count backward from ten, then nothing.

Not feeling any emotion is denial.

Who are you when you turn off the light?

You sleep in order to get up in the morning, do something, feel something, somehow manage to be someone, i.e., you.

Sleep is funny.

You make snuffling noises you would muffle if you were awake.

Do you care?

Doing something is not necessarily doing something on purpose.

Not everyone wants to be ridiculous.

Waking up proves you are not dead.

Not realizing how funny you are is funny.

Serious music is funny in a serious way.

How can music be serious?

Singing, dancing, and playing music is playful, even when the music is serious.

Playing music is more fun than listening to it.

Lighten up is funny.

Take your clothes off is funny.

Serious music-making is beyond funny.

A hole in your pocket is funnier than a hole in your shoe.

You don't have to agree.

Other people don't have to agree with you.

Being funny is not necessarily the answer.

There is no answer, only pain and pleasure, love and loss.

Ouch makes pain funny.

Unnecessary suffering is never funny.

Misery is miserable no matter what you tell yourself.

Pick up the phone and call.

Someone you love wishes the phone would ring.

Just because you can't really help is no reason not to be friendly and encouraging.

Thwarted good will is at least funny.

Someone may be cheered up.

You would be glad to hear from someone.

Harmony requires two voices.

So does drama.

And everything else.

Once you have two, more will enter of their own accord.

What is funny about them may be hidden.

🖐 🖐 🖐

Don't think about the future, or the past.

Feeling feeble is no fun.

Even listening to music gets to be too much trouble.

You know what you mean.

What is so funny about music?

Welcome to the virtual now.

Rain going pitter-patter all over the roof is funny after months of no rain.

When it stops the silence is surprising.

It is funny to close windows that have been open all summer.

It is funny to take fall personally, hard not to.

It is funny to feel cold when you are actually warm.

✋ ✋ ✋

Skin speaks a language everyone can understand.

Not a boundary, planar, it has thickness, variety, and an active inner life.

Part of it is lips and nails.

Not an outer layer of anything, skin is a twenty-pound organ with all of an organ's attributes, just like your liver or your kidneys.

Funny to think of your skin as an organ.

Any silence is rich with inner voices blending into a distinct hum or murmur.

What is it telling you?

What does it want?

You may not want to be funny.

That's understandable.

Life is no joke, etc.

You can only speak for yourself.

Mocking everything is a pretty lame excuse for a personality.

You have to believe something.

Everything is changing although it seems the same.

What are you to believe?

Is it comedy?

Is it intended to be funny?

Is funny even possible anymore?

Well, yes, although it seems ever more difficult to put everything else out of your mind, not to be overwhelmed by compassion for everyone who is suffering needlessly, not to despair for the future of human civilization.

Don't laugh.

Shouldn't you be doing something to help?

Is there anything you can do that actually would help?

Does being funny help?

Is it too late?

Is it too corny to "fiddle while Rome burns"—in order not to cry—to cheer yourself up—to cheer other people up—to spare each other from knowing how you really feel?

Funny is its own best friend.

Laugh because you can.

It is funny to be alive.

Don't wait.

🖐 🖐 🖐

Someday you will be sorry too late.

Sorry is always too late.

Just don't do it.

🖐 🖐 🖐

Antidisestablishmentarianism is still funny.

🖐 🖐 🖐

Sad Sack is funny.

Sad clowns are funny in a lugubrious way.

Feeling sad because it is raining is funny.

Rain is preposterously funny, all that water falling

down out of the sky.

Thunder and lightning are exciting.

Feeling sad is not funny.

Cheer up, things probably could be a lot worse.

And probably will be.

Buster Keaton is funny because he looks so sad.

Lying on the ground and dissolving into the earth's crust is funny.

You barely exist, if at all.

Just existing is a full-time job.

Nothing is left to rise into the empyrean.

You slump like a lifeless doll, no puppeteer gathers up your strings.

No chi.

Get up and do something anyway while you are still alive.

Doing something always makes you feel better.

Doing what you do is funny, like digging a hole and climbing in, or climbing to the top of the mountain.

There you are—now what?

The sun moves across the sky as the square foot of earth you are standing on quietly spins away.

Round and round you go.

Up and down.

Leaves change, people change and stay themselves.

Shadows of the bare branches on the ground show that the leaves have fallen.

Life is funny.

🖐 🖐 🖐

Up is funnier than down.

Woodpeckers are funnier than doves.

The rudeness of crows is funny when it is not annoying.

Annoying is funny also.

Being annoyed at yourself is ridiculous.

How many people do you think you are?

Down is always with you in the form of gravity— hence drugs.

Once you are up you can do something.

Hot air going up ought to be more useful than it is.

Once you are up you can totter along.

Gravity is what makes climbing a mountain so hard.

Gravity makes everything hard, even sleeping, the mattress heavily pressing up against you.

You can't win, but cremation comes close, turning most of you into smoke and gases that rise into the sky and circle the globe forever.

Ashes are easily reabsorbed.

Other smoke may make you high.

Gas may be laughing.

Funnier still is the way sunlight slanting across the wall angularly expresses the revolutions of the spheres.

Everything is moving.

The leaf glowing red on the branch, motionless in the moment of no-wind, falls in an instant, losing what little identity it had.

Is this reality or only a glint from a funny facet of its surface?

Funny how little surfaces express the forms within.

Yet you take them for the thing itself.

All you see of cars, for example, is the skin.

Everything conspires to disguise complexity and multiplicity as simplicity and unity.

That nothing really is what it appears to be is funny all the time.

What is the thing itself if not what you see and touch?

That is the question.

Clouds and snow are visible air.

Potential clouds interpenetrate the air, not air at all but an invisible form of water.

Funny question whether clouds actually exist.

They exist because you see them.

They exist as a stage in a process, appearing from nowhere to dramatize the sky, fabulous forms piling up, infinite shades of grey or layers of brilliant glowing color, disappearing into thin air or lingering, descending, lying on the earth, blurring, dimming, dulling, thickening, gloom itself, darkening the day and human moods, congealing into precipitation, calm and steady or wild and noisy, furiously storming or maintaining their diaphanous sprawl, sailing across the sky like angels.

Actual angels seize upon them as vehicles or embodiments.

Do they take up space or is it all just molecules?

Be funny on your own time.

Be funny for other people.

Be funny because you have nothing else to offer.

Be funny because it is good for you and everyone you know.

Sincerity is key.

Mixing up decades is funny.

Remember the year you started kindergarten?

What else happened?

Who else was there?

You did what you were expected to do.

You tried to understand.

Practice is still the only way to get better.

Look at the funny clothes!

People you knew existed more continuously than others, and in a different way.

Funny how many more people there are now.

No one can keep up.

🖐 🖐 🖐

The last leaves on the tree flutter bravely in the wind, backlit, clinging, red.

Pernicious wind—what a funny idea!

It roars like a herd of animals thundering across the veldt.

You can't do tai chi outdoors when it's like this.

It's like this.

🖐 🖐 🖐

Funny how the days go by, whether or not you are paying attention.

What can you say about them?

This is your life.

You were queen for a day.

When was that?

What happens may crystallize into art or remain in solution and be reabsorbed.

Which is better?

There is already plenty of art, but people still like making it, hoping someone will notice and understand.

What happens to what happens when you are not looking?

There are many people with too little to do but no one to do chores for you.

You have to do them yourself.

Do find someone to hold the ladder.

Falling off a ladder is not funny.

Especially after eighty.

You want to be funny rather than sad.

You want to be light rather than heavy.

Heaviness and sadness can take care of themselves.

Get up and move around.

Roll yourself another joint.

If you are alone, go ahead, talk to yourself

Say anything you like.

No one's feelings will be hurt.

No one will be appalled by your opinions and think you are an asshole.

Later on someone will be there.

Then you can be funny.

Relax.

Let your mind wander.

Be as free as you used to be.

Lose yourself in the moment's momentum.

It's all right if you are not an entomologist.'

You don't have to be anything but yourself.

Let self float away like a blue balloon until it dissolves into the upper air.

You can still exist.

You can still be wherever you are, in the middle of whatever you are in the middle of.

Funny how busy you are, one thing after another and all at once.

Never a dull moment.

Now that it's winter you need to keep warm and dry.

Wet feet are not funny.

Polar exploration was funny until you starved or froze to death.

Even being at home is no sure thing.

Systems can break down.

Everything depends on electricity.

You know next to nothing about power generation and transmission and how things work once you plug them in and what to do when they don't come on.

If your computer dies you can't log on to FAQ.

If your phone dies you can't call tech support.

If your hard drive dies all is lost.

The doctor can't help.

You can't even get an appointment until late next month.

How is this funny?

The past is funny.

You can never get away from it.

The older you are the more you realize your destiny

is not even your own, just another passing incident in an interminable, tightly woven historical epic.

You are more like your father or mother than you like to think, as they were like theirs, and so on back to the Neanderthals, if you are that lucky, increasingly specific as you come closer to modern times, your outlook directly shaped by your grandparents if you knew them, indirectly if not.

Wherever you go, whatever you do, you play your part.

Each of your ancestors was special and unique in much the same way.

People had more fun when you were little in spite of wars, economic collapses, accidents, illnesses, tragic losses, and the rest.

Your father knew how to tell jokes.

Your mother played the violin.

She had a talent for friendship and a taste for interesting people.

Your grandfather did funny tricks, pulling off his thumb, finding quarters in your ear.

You would be funny too if you knew how.

Your grandmother recited poetry and preached

continuous self-improvement.

They all died, and so will you.

Isn't that funny!

Lighten up if you want to be funny.

You want to be happy and wish everybody else could be happy too.

Mindfully.

Does the world just happen to be beautiful and tragic?

God wants you to be funny.

How to be happy.

Do what feels right.

Thinking about it doesn't help.

You already know how you feel.

Thinking is more likely to mislead.

Thinking tries to justify what you have already decided.

Not thinking is probably worse.

You don't have to justify yourself, just try to

remember that your post-European-Enlightenment mindset is not the only way of looking at the world.

Unconscious preconceptions are funny.

Funny means worth thinking about.

Then you are happy.

🖐 🖐 🖐

Funny how much you have forgotten—everything, really.

You were there, how can you not remember?

All you remember is a few of the facts, and most of them are wrong.

Or a feeling or potential feeling, or an atmosphere or style, not even what music was playing.

Everything you and everyone else said and did has vanished into thin air.

Years pass.

Then what?

Maybe the past doesn't matter.

But it does.

What else is more important?

The future never arrives, and the present continually

slips away, creating more past all the time.

What were you doing five minutes ago?

Sitting here reading.

Ha ha.

At the same time listening to music, thinking about marinating the salmon, biting a fingernail, frowning, scratching different parts of your body, squirming in your chair, no telling what else.

Is squirming funnier or less funny than wiggling?

And what are you thinking?

Are you thinking?

How funny is that?

Same with anything.

Little wonder you can't remember anything specific about what it was like to make love when you were young.

Or old.

All that intensity.

Gone.

Yearning for satisfaction.

Rain is like music after months of silence.

Falling is the fading light, funny and sad.

You are neither here nor there, perpetually poised between irreconcilable funny states of mind and body, torn between widely separated times and places, living and loving in wildly different ways.

This quiet rain so soothing nothing else matters.

After that something else will happen.

Try to be ready when it does.

Then something else.

You want it to be funny.

You need to laugh.

Oh but the rain is funny enough, murmuring droplets scattered across the skylight on the playful breath of wind.

You had forgotten.

Dogs may think barking is funny but they sound serious.

It sounds as though they are suffering.

You wonder why you didn't notice sooner.

You didn't want to, or the dog wasn't barking.

It isn't the dog's fault.

The dog didn't ask to exist.

You feel yourself becoming angry at the owners for going away all day leaving the dog tied up.

Neighbors are funny.

Better not say too much.

How not to be funny.

Everyone you know has thoughts, fragmentary, continually interrupted.

You try to follow along although you are not sure you truly understand where they are coming from or what they are trying to say.

You certainly don't want to argue.

You want to argue but don't want to sound grumpy.

You would rather be funny than put out half-baked opinions of your own.

It might be nice to be serious once in a while.

You smile encouragingly at your friend's incoherent jumble of good intentions, looking serious when it seems more appropriate.

The situation is serious but you don't want to be serious.

What's the point?

It is horribly funny how helplessly people reason.

Complex forces vastly stronger than human will interact with no regard for personal thoughts and feelings.

Still you try.

Funny the way music frees the mind to move.

One part listens, another part dances, another part thinks.

Time tangibly expands.

The present breathes.

Anything is possible.

Imagination is the first appearance of reality.

Everything begins as a kind of dream.

Remembering is a pleasure and a privilege.

It was not exactly funny, not exactly, but it made an impression.

You knew it at the time.

Then everything else happened, just as you hoped it would.

Or not.

Music, though, is something else, attack, decay, the moment receding the moment it arrives, the rhythm promising unlimited continuity, forgetting its extinction.

Rain on the roof too, the same and always new.

It is funny to still be alive and think of being dead.

Not existing will be the final irony, no gesture possible when you can no longer move.

No one will recognize the humor of the situation, if nothing happening is a situation.

You will not be there.

Dead people often reappear in dreams of the living, but you can't count on it.

The old feelings arise still unresolved.

The old regrets.

You are there almost as much as you ever were.

Do you exist if no one knows you?

No one living knows what this moment reminds you

of, which no one else remembers.

All that dies with you.

It was already tenuous.

If that isn't funny, you don't know what is.

You feel warm and fuzzy.

It is very nice.

Some days you are in rare form.

Everything is funny and surprising.

You laugh in the face of disappointment.

How frustrating people are!

But it's not your problem!

Something has to be there, it might as well be this.

You can reason yourself into euphoria.

And reason is not the only way.

Try whirling like a dervish.

Try thinking like an owl after a good meal.

The ticking stove reminds you of passing time and all the funny things you have to do.

Suddenly the days are short.

The pendulum swings.

🖐 🖐 🖐

Night is not dark.

The electricity still works.

Fires are burning.

Last flies appear.

Votes are being counted.

It isn't funny anymore.

🖐 🖐 🖐

Sticky fingers are funnier than heavy pockets.

Music is prettier than art.

Dubious declarations take the place of truth.

Truth is whatever needs to be said.

Meanwhile the world.

People are suffering.

Beauty coexists with hunger, pain, and loss.

Triviality is obsolete.

Being funny is a last resort.

Nastiness is not funny.

Love is funny!

🖐 🖐 🖐

Darkness falls and all lie down.

Darkness departs and all rise if they still can.

Everyone in your time zone is doing the same funny things on the same rhythm, rising and falling like a wave circling the globe.

Now you are running around, now you are still.

Now tapping on a keyboard, now nodding off.

Now peering at a screen, now asleep.

Now awake, now dreaming.

Now alert, now dull.

Now entangled, now alone.

Funny how it all goes on.

🖐 🖐 🖐

When the jet booms over, the goat jumps.

It would be funny if it weren't so annoying.

Where can you escape to when you need to escape?

The laugh track ruins your enjoyment.

Mean people take over your town.

All is not lost until it is.

The horse thinks the cable is a snake and crashes

into the cactus.

It looks funny, but the stunt man winds up in the hospital.

Who should be surprised?

Decades later it makes a good story—laughs, compassion, a lesson learned.

What is the lesson?

You practice lest you forget.

Your weaknesses become your strengths.

What is the joke that goes with this punchline?

Thinking about the future is funny, as if the present were not funny enough.

You still have the rest of the day, time for everything.

No surprises, please, to disrupt your expectations.

You need to be there.

Sail steadily forward, like the afternoon of a faun, or Daphnis and Chloe in the rain.

Take the immediate situation into consideration.

The past is over.

Nothing is ever really over.

Ergo farce.

🖐 🖐 🖐

How to be funny.

Is playful and light-hearted the same thing as funny?

Scarlatti is often funny.

Beethoven is more often serious.

🖐 🖐 🖐

Serious pain is not funny.

Serious pain takes you over and thins you out.

You can't think about anything else.

To a child the least little pain is tragic.

Later you get used to it.

You may even laugh about it.

When it's over you forget it.

It's hard to be funny, though, while you are wincing, gasping, or nagged by a throbbing ache.

🖐 🖐 🖐

You will be funny later.

You will think of a funny story to tell.

Something happened, people reacted, ridiculous consequences ensued.

It happens all the time.

You were one of the actors, you must be able to remember.

Everybody laughed.

It was really very funny.

You should have been there.

And you were.

How can anything be funny?

Your species is fatally flawed.

The situation is a complete fiasco.

Seriously.

The basic character of your life is threatened along with everyone else.

The prospects of human civilization look worse every day.

Still you love.

You are the heart of the world, radiating love in all directions, fading with distance but extending to infinity.

All people.

Cats and dogs and other animals.

All beings.

Fantastic images arise spontaneously inside your mind, some of them unexpectedly funny.

Where do they come from?

What can they teach you?

Taking a break is a funny idea.

You can't take a break from existing.

Most of what you do is self-prescribed according to well-known principles and conditioning.

A small part is free at the best of times.

You are free to work if you choose to think of it that way.

You can have a room of your own if you insist.

Even so, everybody needs a break once in a while.

The boss will send you home if you look funny, if you sound desperate, if you are about to flip out.

That would not be funny.

What will you do on your break, go to Italy, or more of the same?

You could swim out to the float and scream.

You could sit in your chair and write, page after funny page.

Is anything funny except what is?

Or is everything funny if you think it is?

Do you even know what funny means?

What are you looking for?

Self is not only a prison, of course.

Self is what plays.

Self can be funny.

You can enjoy yourself.

You can be as crude or subtle as you please.

You can absorb and reflect a cosmic abundance of impressions.

You can be happy though sad and sad though happy.

You are partly at least a figment of your own imagination.

Imagination is a bodily function.

You are the body and in the body.

Beyond body you are an idea released into the universe, dissipating into distance, disappearing into time.

You might as well be funny.

Be yourself, you can't help it, this is it!

Be as free as you can.

Good reasons exist not to be free but self is not one of them.

You yourself are already gone, this is extra.

How to be funny.

Cross your eyes.

Stick out your tongue.

Stick your thumbs in your ears and waggle your fingers.

Is that still funny?

How to be funny non-stupidly.

Puns.

Frivolous remarks.

Unselfconscious cheerfulness.

Fatalism.

Stoicism.

Empiricism.

Epicureanism.

Existentialism.

Practical jokes.

Musical jokes.

Physical jokes.

Light-hearted contrariness.

Locate the humor lurking in every exchange and let it out.

Be good to yourself.

Be good.

Funny doesn't have to actually be funny.

Funny is good.

🖐 🖐 🖐

Reconsider the whole idea of being funny.

You want to be serious.

You want to think about politics.

Is there anything else?

Your very existence depends on everything working.

Imagine living with a ruined infrastructure, starving, sick, attacked from above.

That would not be funny.

That would be reality.

You would rather not.

You would rather be funny.

You would rather be warm and well fed, with an insulated house and money in the bank.

Enjoy it while it is still funny.

Have a few laughs with people you like.

Go ahead.

🖐 🖐 🖐

People are naturally funny.

You don't have to practice.

You have to practice not being funny.

It is hard work taking yourself seriously.

Inner blockages have developed, a habit of self-editing.

You are worried that being funny is not serious.

If you really want to be funny, you still can.

You don't have to tell jokes, you can think of a funny story and write it up as a play.

Invite your friends over for a potluck, drink wine, assign parts, and act it out.

Funny how raking up the big wet walnut leaves on a chilly bright December afternoon last year you thought this might be the last time, and then it came around again, and here you are, not even minding, feeling better this year, stronger, thanks to regular exercise, good habits, and good health, God willing, knowing there's no need to push yourself and be miserable, you can do part of it today and stop, throw down the rake, go inside, sit down, warm your hands, take a break before tai chi, and rake some more another day.

You yearn for something besides funny.

You have a wider range of potential feelings than that.

Embrace them all.

Bring them into the light.

You don't have to do anything about them.

They are who you really are.

Action is not required.

Love them, endure them.

Disguises are funny.

Who are you pretending to be now?

No one is fooled.

A man in a spotlight in a dark crowded room calls you "Judge" as you find your way to the bathroom.

Most of the audience turns to look at you and laughs.

You are secretly charmed.

"Judge"?

That's comedy.

Like a flute and tabla playing together.

The music goes on for hours.

It doesn't have to be funny, it can be anything you like, "funny," "tempestuous," "intoxicated," "blissed out."

The music is oblivious to what you call it..

Time slows.

The stars come out again.

It takes nerve to sustain the Adagio, which has nothing to do with funny.

Any second you will make a mistake.

Still, you try.

Time is tangible, magnetic, adhesive—loosening and catching the beat.

Every phrase refers to one underlying pattern.

It is you yourself, one of billions floating in the flowing fluid of becoming.

Music is a mirror, how you look to yourself an artifact.

No longer trying to be funny, you hover suspended in a web of melody and harmony, rhythm and flow, order and spontaneity, poised to realize what you knew all along.

Half an hour is forever.

If you're not funny, you don't know what is.

Life has put on the lineaments of tragedy.

If you could change the course of history, you might be able to think about something else.

Retroactively.

Art bares inner truth, which needs room to breathe.

Great gulping gasps would be more appropriate than this calm and steady in and out.

Steadiness and equilibrium are all you can hope for.

Still the fire burns within.

The paper charred to ash collapses into powder, the possibility of laughter bright in the vanishing words.

Funny you should ask, and the story follows.

The rejected twin returns as a serpent.

You are not sure you know what's going on.

Maybe nothing, you hope.

Everything is a one-time event, nothing happens again, however much it appears to, creeping imperceptibly forward until something else takes its place.

You no longer long for change.

The serpent-self is your long-lost sister-brother, pending gender assignment.

Whatever is will be.

🖐 🖐 🖐

How can you possibly be funny?

You are too tired.

You are too old.

You are not all that well.

You are poor.

You are sober.

You meant to say something else.

You meant to say something more cheerful.

You meant to be funny.

What is funny anyway?

Funny is misconstrued misinformation, upended expectations, catastrophic slip-ups.

Funny is wearing stripes, plaids, and polka dots.

Dancing the polka is funny.

Making fun of yourself is potentially funny.

Being funny is funny.

Falling down drunk used to be funny.

Dropping a metal tray stacked high with dishes is funny.

Someone is embarrassed, someone is fired, someone is funny, someone dies.

Being alive is funnier than being dead.

Dead people have few opportunities to be funny.

There is nothing wrong with being funny.

Sometimes it is the only right thing to do.

Other times you don't realize how funny you are.

People are too embarrassed to laugh.

Perhaps you insist on being taken seriously.

No one knows the difference.

Is there a difference?

There must be.

Everything is different from everything else.

Nothing is the same as anything else.

Yet you are genetically all but identical with every other member of homo sapiens.

You do the same thing every day, with minor adjustments and gradual evolution, until you can't do it anymore, just like everybody else.

You don't dare even try to be funny.

What if you can't?

🖐 🖐 🖐

Of course you can.

You have to believe that.

Cut off one thing, pretty soon there is nothing left.

No telling what will happen after that.

Your lost sense of humor may return.

You need a kitchen table for your sense of humor to sit down at.

You can be funny even if you are not Jewish.

A little funny, a faint smile, perhaps, a little brighter outlook.

🖐 🖐 🖐

Gurdjieff is one of the great jokester wise men.

The same funny ideas bubble up wherever you look.

They are not kidding.

You take it on.

From there it is only upward.

The mountain path of slow collapse.

Ideas will help you if you can think of them when you need them.

You are referring to the dentist's chair?

What would Buddha do?

Your mind is attached to the point of the pick.

Another person's hands inside your mouth is funny.

You put up with it.

Funny how everything is constructed of tinier and tinier bits.

Tiny details lead to gigantic ideas.

The fine view is funny, the wide view frightening.

What do you take for granted vs. actually observe?

What do you imagine is shared vs. actually your own?

How can you possibly convey your comfort with the common vs. your appreciation of the special?

Can you have a conversation across languages?

What is to be said?

Do you know how to say it?

Being in the same room is not quite enough.

Something must happen.

You must manifest your funny ways.

You must appreciate the funny things the other person does and says.

Now you are having fun!

✋ ✋ ✋

Must you be so serious?

Admit you are funny, let people laugh at you.

So what if it's rainy and cold?

Do you have the answer?

Probably not, but that doesn't have to stop you.

You are not called upon to save the world single-handed.

That's asking too much of a song.

✋ ✋ ✋

How to be funny.

Answer the telephone.

It might be someone you like.

Or someone you didn't expect to hear from.

It makes you happy to hear the beloved voice.

This is close enough to being funny.

Maybe better.

Even so it is not the same thing.

You feel like the last fly exploring the surface of the desk.

Wood is different from plastic.

You know it by feeling it with your sticky feet.

You fly away and immediately come back.

This is the time for doing what you are doing now.

Learning to be funny.

Learning to be interesting out of the corner of someone's eye.

How fast can you be funny?

Ten minutes?

Ten minutes is 14,400 frames.

Comic confusion requires elaborate planning.

People practice for years.

Being funny is hard work.

Hard work can be fun without being funny.

Soft work you can relax and fall into.

Then it's just a matter of opening the file and tapping away.

Tapping is funny all by itself.

You find yourself smiling.

🖐 🖐 🖐

Considering what happens, do you even want to be funny?

Soul is more to the point.

Harmony is the point, always changing, so satisfying when it resolves.

Anticipation is the point.

Something may happen, and you may happen to be paying attention when it does.

Attention is the real point.

Attention is the real you.

Otherwise you are walking around in a fog.

Something funny may happen.

You may not notice.

Not everything depends on how you look at it.

Some things happen anyway.

They can be funny too.

Is that something you are willing to accept?

If so, you are ready to begin.

You hear the fly fly, the quick throbbing hum of fly wings.

It's that quiet.

It's a funny sound in the charged-up silence.

When the silent house creaks in the night or the refrigerator suddenly grumbles, you are frightened, thinking someone else is there.

Probably not, but what if?

That would be a surprise.

Turn a corner and someone is there.

They might kill you for no reason.

Stranger things have happened.

Other people's purposes are never entirely clear.

They might be desperate, or devotees of some cruel god, or seeking revenge for something you did or didn't do.

They might be selling something funny that you don't want.

You are glad no one is there.

You are happy to be alone.

You are happy someone is sleeping in the other room.

People talking is funny.

How can they have so much to say day after day?

The best way to be funny is without trying.

Or without realizing it.

When you find out, you feel like a fool.

Being a fool is funny.

You don't have to do anything.

Others will do it for you if you are nice.

Another funny thing is the way people are not what you expect.

You imagine a soul-mate.

You imagine understanding.

Instead the person you meet has no idea what you are open to.

You imagine romance or hot sex, at least lively conversation.

It is not like that.

They are in their own box which does not appeal to you at all.

You wonder what their story is but not really.

You wanted to reveal yourself.

No one is interested.

No surprises.

What's funny is that you expected something else.

※ ※ ※

You can't stand being tickled.

Trying to funny is no excuse.

※ ※ ※

Sitting up straight and breathing is funny.

Set aside time to exist.

Millions of others are doing the same thing (the *sangha*).

Time is one dimension, space another.

Your skull contains universes expanding in all directions in the vast unknown.

Straighten up and continue to breathe.

Don't stop until you do.

Pulsation is the funny way life keeps going.

Random variation is the key to pattern formations.

Rhythm is basic.

Masturbation is funny.

You can learn all about it on the internet.

What would you do all day without the internet?

No one else has to be there.

You are complete.

You come, then you come back.

Sometimes you laugh, thinking that was exactly what you wanted to do right then.

And why not?

But why bother?

Dependable pleasure.

Nothing more relaxing.

Wake up the sex brain.

Stop thinking about everything else.

Make sure you still can.

Then you can think again.

Two-word phrases are funny.

Frantic lizards.

Paused consciousness.

Normal deviation.

🖐 🖐 🖐

Fortunately, housework is funny too.

You are forever picking things up, folding things, putting things away.

The floor needs sweeping.

Laundry piles up.

Your position is that you like washing dishes.

Putting out the trash is funny.

No getting away from it.

Not because life is unbearably tragic otherwise, as per Kierkegaard.

You don't have to think that way until tragedy strikes you.

In the meantime you can be funny.

Inwardly is not enough.

Let it be seen.

🖐 🖐 🖐

Gravitational waves are funny.

You imagine yourself riding them in a little boat or tub.

How real is that?

Clouds of widely spaced atoms dim more distant stars and galaxies.

You prefer to be at home.

How funny it is to do precisely what you intended!

The clock could look to you for the time.

You are the true thermometer.

You bask in the illusion of being still.

Music is not always funny.

Life is not always fun.

Poor you!

Charm is not enough.

You want to get up out of your chair and dance.

The day is young.

No, actually, the day is coming to an end.

The clouds are suddenly pink.

It gives you a funny feeling.

How to be funny.

What is to be done?

You still don't know.

What are you looking for?

What have you found so far?

After what just happened, you are a different person.

You can never go back.

Would you even want to?

Are you getting the idea?

This is how to be funny.

It works for you.

Ten minutes go by before you know it.

What was funny before is no longer funny.

Everything changed before your eyes.

You were thinking about something else.

That too is valid and worth thinking about.

You have to be funny in a whole new way.

You have two minutes left.

What's funny about laughing gas is to wake up not knowing anything has happened.

It is hard to throw things away, but once you do, it doesn't matter anymore.

Isn't everything like that?

Nothing is funny about war.

Not being able to bear watching the news is a relief.

There is nothing you can do about it anyway except press on, be kind, generous, and grateful, love everyone, help where you can, sympathize, keep the faith, read good books, and hope for better days.

You can still be funny.

You can't help being funny.

Obviously not everything will be funny, no matter how funny you are.

Stay out of the way of war if you possibly can.

War destroys funniness and every good thing.

Resist with every bone in your body.

Isn't it funny how time flies and you fly right along with it.

Music makes this clear as long as it keeps keeping on.

When the music stops everything else keeps going but you are less capable of being funny.

The bell rings, and you notice you are breathing.

The bell rings again and you do something else.

Sentences are funny.

Commas may or may not appear.

🖐 🖐 🖐

Turning off the radio lets you think.

Thoughts are not the net of words.

Once caught they are no longer free.

Funny how ideas get inside your skin.

Your mind is whirling even as your body is still.

What are you waiting for?

You are the spinner.

🖐 🖐 🖐

Meditation is funny.

You sit there breathing.

That's really all there is to it.

How long before you forget what you are doing (meditating) and start thinking about something else?

That's the trick.

It sounds easy but it isn't.

Everyone agrees it is highly beneficial if you do it every day.

So do it.

Pick a place.

Carve out the time.

Ten or fifteen minutes is enough.

If you don't have ten or fifteen minutes you are moving too fast.

Isn't it funny how ready you are to believe that something perfectly simple is impossible?

Some days nothing is funny.

You can't imagine anything ever being funny.

Seriousness takes over.

People bring up deep thoughts and feelings and talk

about them seriously.

Terrible things are happening, as is so often the case.

You avoid talking about the news.

The present is the climax of everything that has come before so it is worse now than ever.

Nothing funny about it.

You can't live like that.

You can be funny.

You can be serious.

You live in love.

Love God, love peace, love family and friends, love all beings, love the world, love what you know and don't know, love yourself, love your life, love the one you love.

How to be funny.

Ask yourself.

Look inside and look around.

No one else can be funny for you just as no one else can be you.

You are free unless you are not.

Your heart goes out to everyone in bondage, sick, cold, hungry, lost, all in need and jeopardy, and those in peril on the sea.

Breath is shared, blood is not.

Stripes and polka dots are still funny.

Insist if you must.

Some people don't think they can possibly be funny.

Most don't care one way or the other.

They have their own funny lives.

Would they be funnier if you knew more?

Or less funny?

Must they be funny?

How about you?